HIGH ERRATIC ECOLOGY
Julia Rose Lewis

KFS

Newton-le-Willows

Published in the United Kingdom in 2020
by The Knives Forks And Spoons Press,
51 Pipit Avenue,
Newton-le-Willows,
Merseyside,
WA12 9RG.

ISBN 978-1-912211-63-0

Acknowledgements:

Poems from this book appeared in the following exhibits and
publications: Museum of Futures (2018), Poem Brut at Spike Island
(2018), Museum of Futures (2017), *Datableed, Lighthouse Magazine,
Amberflora, Erotoplasty, Hippocrates Initiative Anthology* (2018),
*Burning House Press, HVTN, Visual Verse, The Learned Pig, Backlash,
Volta Anthology, Enchanting Verses, Poetry Wales.*

My deepest gratitude to Annabel Banks, Idha Toft Valeur, Olga
Kolesnikova, SJ Fowler for allowing me to include our collaborations
in this book.

Supported using public funding by

**ARTS COUNCIL
ENGLAND**

LOTTERY FUNDED

dedicated to SJ Fowler

Table of Contents

THE THEME WITH THE TOOTSIE ROLL EARS

MACHAIRODUS APHANISTUS ...

FOLLOW THAT SHIP

METABOLIC AND COMMUNITY SYNERGY OF ORAL BACTERIA IN COLORECTAL CANCER

RE: MISSION

HEARING FROGS AND KINGS

LET THERE BE A BEAR AND A LISTENER

THE THEME WITH THE TOOTSIE ROLL EARS

Pooka I

pooka poke at this
beast of pookae the pookae
take pookam to pooka

Fair creature, change your shape again. Goblin as bucca as wolf as pwca horse as pouque as goat pouquelée as cat as poulpiquet as raven dark thing see horse the girl stole away with in the Minstrel's Tale. We thought our beast would be in the first declension in latin, the first nouns we learned were road and girl. Changer of shapes, now pounce on the high ghost of girlhood. We played as jesters in the court of a pregnant king, once and future writers. No jokes dear creature, with dessert, we will do gymnastics. We will remember when we were screeching your name in the cavern, the echoes bouncing against the high hills of human speech.

Pooka II

smell ammonia,
waiting for a bag of lime
all the themes watching

Magpie blinked at me. The theme with your ears dear pooka. Your ride, best trip, but remember their fear of baby fingers and fluttering ribbons. Yellow was corn, third place at bridle wild. Always, this line I know, pushing out one more theme.

Returning to black rock, I cleaned the paddock of a pony that should have been dog food already. I cleaned the paddock of a chestnut thoroughbred that would not have been taken even for glue. Both are ghosts of that Mad Hatter theme.

Surveying my work from the upper paddock, I was waiting. Magpie sidled up the fence watching, waiting, commiserating. She brought her barrel in line with my legs. She blinked at me. I climbed on this theme. No martingale, no saddle, no bridle, no boots, and no hardhat, we were naked. She walked and I wound my fingers in the white. All the danger, sitting under those low wood beams, and yet, glad. Winning, when my oldest-youngest friend smiled wide.

Greatheart – va, va ou j'y vais. Go, go, take me where I'm going on the honor of the pooka, I say. Carry me home on the back of a midsummer night's dream.

Dear Bear,

you held me in sun-
light nervous so shiny as
black patent leather.

Dear phorophyte, you have held me in the light. Fair play, the apple-shaped pear is not to reunite as sinister. Neither bear nor Rottweiler, the skin on a ripe Asian pear has the color of a Rottweiler's points.

Let me be epinephrine not a parasite. Play fair against the loss of neurons that secrete norepinephrine in the sympathetic nervous system. Fearing the shuffling trot, like a horse with navicular changes, so goes the Parkinsonian gait. You might as well ride a bear or a Rottweiler.

So just fault the three year old for calling a Rottweiler a bear; the traditional gait of the Rottweiler is the trot. A prototype of oil slick black fur, my prayer to the bear, the peer, and the phorophyte: let us pause on the lawn before the line of trees.

Pooka III

dear unripe orange
demon of the forest words
to the woods for rest

The farmer's lamed horse that referred to the tootsie roll horse with the huge ears, my early love, part pooka. Mare means theme means horse here. Horses are another species of epiphyte.

The shapeshifter, Sheba was mistaken, the noses of horses are dry. The wet was a vestige of the canid, another preferred form pookarum.

Mere, just see the sea. I am jumping up and down at the sight of them on the ferry, returning to a teenage girl, returning to the Rottweiler idea. In summer we live with the sound and a little bit of land between us.

Pookae take the same markings as Rottweilers, golden rabbit against black rabbit too. He is cool and I am furry.

Thunder and lightening and shadows, how brain-damaged am I to forget the family black Labrador Retriever? Walking the mid-island with Shadow. Thunder and light to lull us all to sleep tonight.

Hieratic I
After Dad Dr. Anne Dalke

red delicious
the malus domestica
worth a thousand words

Recite it meant, oh my god, she's so Quaker! Despite the giant turtle earring, and the shirt red as apple: anthocyanin, all American, and sinister. I have seen her sitting barefoot on lab bench and on the facing bench. She gave me the planting of apple trees in the fall as a metaphor for depression. For of course, old horses turn into trees, a farm of a forest. A story of evolution. Appetite is a horse called Apple, who thinks herself to be a cow and steals a calf. Let me be an epiphyte not a parasite in this evolution of stories.

Pooka IV

the tootsie roll theme
came out of the dam theme mare
to filly before

The point of the trick was that I trusted her. I loved that mare, and her fairy magic took the form of falling from her sometimes and not getting hurt. A little evil, I would lay in the mud. Sinking into the cold sand and manure, staining my clothes, until my mother pulled me up.

To ride a pooka is a treat.

I learned to ride a theme, like listening to poetry in a foreign language, all there is is rhythm, rhyme, and cognates. Coming out of the corner, I squared my shoulders. As soon as I could see the fence through her great ears, I closed my eyes. Age of the changeling opposite of fear. This was no floppy eared frame, that came out of dressage; she was supposed to be a three-day eventer, like her dam. True care, she was unlucky. I was a dozen different kinds, truth brings.

To trust equals to love all the very beast.

Part Mother

Remember the manure and the rubber. When I was young and upset you would send me out into the ring to pick up poop. Remember the mustard brown and the drab rubber. So much depended upon saving the rubber that was already recycled from car tires. The horses and riders were following the track in the footing. Remember the mustard and the drab. Barn swallows would dive bomb the manure looking for undigested grains; while the horses and riders circled the ring. Remember the mustard seeds and the titanium. All I had was the pitch fork with the plastic tines for mucking stalls with shavings. Remember the mushrooms, the brooms, the muck tubs, the wide and lightweight shovel. There was an unlit loft with tightly packed bales, a slippery floor, and splinters as sharp as hay. Remember the stainless steel. The needle of the clock is the lunge line in your hand though the fingers have grown thick with age. Later you pick the hay from my hair and I am your little girl.

remember trying
to separate brown from gray
background mosaic

I have nightmares about needing to go out there to clean is to tell you I love you.

Hieratic II

My dear apple,
I steal the color of falling leaves,
my dear pear.

The pah, the pinch pressing so sure,
the reading is intimidating
a slice of apple is held behind the lobe
for ear piercing at home.

My host tree,
who is one-half the holding pattern, I want
to feed you a pear,
slice by slice, you see a volunteer appear?

Still this classroom, an earring catechesis
and a call to prayer,
steal this classroom, time and imagination indeed.

The Bajoran earring is a symbol of faith
and family, my ideal reader,
my present from the arts gods, this is deep space indeed.

Planting apple trees in the fall, the cognitive unconscious
is a compost pile, the fruits of the present tense.
I steal apples from the woman in the orange jacket
at my roommate's garden party.
I steal pears from the man in the Nantucket-red pants
at the gallery event.

MACHAIRODUS APHANISTUS
(FELIDAE, MACHAIRODONTINAE, HOMOTHERINI)
FROM THE LATE MIOCENE

(Vallesian, MN10) site of Batallones-3
(Torrejón de Velasco, Madrid, Spain)
Marcos F. G. Monescilloa, Manuel J. Salesaa,
Mauricio Antóna, Gema Siliceoa
& Jorge Moralesa

What You Leave Behind

are teeth the diamonds of the skeleton,
their denser mineralization
leads to the tall M1 paracone that cuts
to wear and tear the meat,
a wear groove
that gives in the anterolateral face,
do not look a god's gift in the mouth
and take measurement of the m1 talonid.

"Traumastocyonine pattern, however is created by the tall M1 paracone that cuts a wear groove in the anterolateral face of the m1 talonid."

Grinding Down

behind the M1 metacone
not quite as tall as the paracone
cuts to wear and tear the pinecone.
A prominent wear surface says white wish bone,
says would a bear eat a honey-flavored ice-cream cone
on the anterolateral face of the moon?
Past all of the m2 trigonid (a facet is also cut by the metacone,
metaphor runs down the posteroexternal corner of the stone
of the m1 talonid just below the m1 hypoconid) alone.

"Behind this facet the M1 metacone, not quite as tall as the paracone, cuts
a prominent wear surface on the anterolateral face of the m2 trigonid (a
facet is also cut by the metacone down the posteroexternal corner of the
m1 talonid just below the m1 hypoconid)."

Hieratic III

Let me be an epiphyte, not a parasite. Let me be one epiphyte, not a parasite. Let me be one epiphyte, a part of this forest. Let me be an epiphyte, not a parasite a part of the rest. Let me be epinephrine, not a parasite. Let me be an epiphyte, let us not repeat fine, if forest green is hunter green with blue here. Let me not be a parasite. Let me tell you of the blue light of labradorite in your eyes, even that night. Once upon a tree a plant.

Holding Two Strands

I dreamed that my teeth turned to
labradorite, they were beautiful, finally,

the tall M2 paracone creates
through circling and tearing the fauna it meets

a wear groove on the outer face
I face, the clear rubber of the m2 shines

between no fangs its trigonid
and talonid no more fangs.

"Finally, the tall M2 paracone creates a wear groove on the outer face of
the m2 between its trigonid and talonid."

With Respect to the Boiling Water

do not overcook the plastic,
the elevated, the massive m1 hypoconid fits
in its bites
firmly, but not all the way through the mouthguard
into the M1 moving from London from Leeds from
protocone basin:
again, a dental read older than old mortar-
pestle-like hardness to oxycodone,,,
slip end device.

"The elevated massive m1 hypoconid fits firmly into the M1 protocone basin: a dental mortar-pestle device."

Seriously Jolly Fan[1]

You found me in the suburbs, where beautiful is that a
black scorpion can appear light blue under a black light.
twinning surface within   See labradorite-like arachnid
the rock scorpions or burrowing scorpions?   parallel
surfaces   Not every stone was a little pond falling from
the hand.   very fine platelets   So just fault the hairy
scorpions or thick-tailed scorpions?   passes through the
stone   "Not every forest/ was a brittle lake horizontal."
displays blue reflections   The tall experiment is
walking towards creeping scorpions or tree scorpions?
refracting   Tall inclusions of ilmenite, rutile, magnetite,
fight tall scorpions or pale-legged scorpions?
inclusions   The cabochon stone was a bit of pond scum
was a brittle pool horizontal.   sometimes fracturing
Skittering over the currents of rainwater, the branch is
about the shape of a scorpion about to sting the thinking skin.

---

[1] From SJ Fowler's poem, 'The forest of animals where humans aren't welcome'

Leading to

the high hum m2 trigonid
is focused to an edge formed by its protconid-metaconid:
this edge fits in between the posterior border,
it is forbidden to look the gift of the arts god in the M1;
and the anterior border
shall follow metamorphosis to the west
of Strood of M2, and on the heel of them ahem the M2
is applied to the shallow protocone,
take the basin of the M2 for Sheerness and Maidstone East.

"The high m2 trigonid is focused to an edge formed by its protconid-metaconid: this edge fits between the posterior border of M1 and the anterior border of M2, and the heel of the m2 is applied to the shallow protocone basin of the M2."

Bit of Apple Flavored Rubber

that the three primary worry,
they tear the flora and fauna to wear grooves found

on these the m1-2 are cut by tall,
nearly all vertical fences and flat labial cusps,

up the diagonal down the outside,
up the diagonal down the outside

of the M1-2, I would ride it in a D-ring happy mouth
and let it constitute the essence of the Thaumastocyonine Pattern.

"The three primary wear grooves found on the m1-2 are cut by tall, nearly vertical labial cusps of the M1-2 and constitute the essence of the "thaumastocyonine" pattern."

FOLLOW THAT SHIP

Hieratic IV

Audrey Hepburn is
playing twister with a chameleon.

This is not fair play, my lady,
right hand to red a minor god reads
from where the needle stops,
and Audrey puts on a red leather glove.

The red circles are crepuscular
suns running across six of the universes.

Audrey needs the gloves to handle the sun.

The twenty four circles are not
necessarily from the same universes.

The blue circles are
the oceans across six of the universes.

A chameleon prays, 'let me tell you
of the blue light of labradorite in your eyes,
even that night.'

Audrey smiles, and lifts her left hand
to give a chameleon a pat
before resting on the blue circle.

Left foot to yellow is a gift

from the citrus god to remind
a chameleon of the all the lemons trees
waiting for their old world lizard to return.

This makes a chameleon smile.

The yellow circles are
the days across six of the universes.

The needle sticks on right foot green, once
for Audrey, once for a chameleon.

Green is under the skin, the yellow
upper layer of the chromophores plus
the blue lower layer of the chromophores
plus the temperature.

A chameleon tries to feel green
and turns beautiful.

Audrey is already
beautiful trying to reach the green.

What is the matter: in the multiverse
a chameleon has won a game of twister
with Audrey Hepburn.

Gift from the Citrus God

lemon on lemon
on citrus tower ringing
at a place: treasure

I want to feed a chameleon a lemon. The anatomy of a chameleon's tongue is imitating the arm of a boxer. Imagine eyes without corners. A chameleon can see visible and ultraviolet light and the latter seems to stimulate them to bask and to feed. So let a chameleon rotate its eyes to see its tail turn into lemon peel. I want to watch a chameleon's head turn light yellow and white and bright yellow, to watch the wave move down its londonite body. Chameleons can get parasites including the protozoans that cause sleeping sickness and malaria. Let me be an epiphyte not a parasite. I want to feed a chameleon a lemon slice by slice by hell by highly longing tongue. All lemons are bound to fall down, some lemons are better to feed a chameleon.

Follow the Drunken Molly

born in disaster
her midwife was warrior
alien and friend

Dear Atlas, dear transporter chief, dear chief of operations of the starship Defiant, you are Tinker and Terran even in the mirror universe. You killed one of the fire-cave aliens to protect your family. I will just leave this here as lived elements must be, because I still do not know what it means when an elemental poet says beautiful. Let me be an epiphyte, let us not repeat fine, if forest green is hunter green with blue here. I name the space between trees and elements a duonetic field. Paradise in part, because the forests surrounding the village are filled with astatine deposits, dear phorophyte. I name you miles.

Continue to Follow the Drunken Molly

the drunken Molly
leans into passing traffic
as sliding glass doors

Please see the sober Molly for the photographs as one half of our series of postcards from posh reading venues. Think of dress uniforms. Think of pauses as periods as pips added to collars, where the history of your rank is problematic. I am just going to leave trials and tribble-elations here. A pet tarantula named Christina whispers of a morbid fear of spiders, and later, honor among thieves results in you adopting a cat. You can not resist your own generosity. In order to assist a Tosk you disobey direct orders from the commander of the space station and receive a note on your record and he regrets writing it, more than you regret receiving it. We learn that you are literate in the trill language in 'Prodigal Daughter'.

Ihadafriend Continued

it's only a cucumber moon,
this rind. Around mother nature thin and deed,
of course I have not read her letters. I am leaving them until the end
takes after her. Turning baristas into sheep,

this string around mother nature.
Exchanging Facebook messages with my supervisor late Saturday. Night
after taking her turning baristas into messengers,
the tall plant adds a nitrogen to fried. To get a friend

exchanging Facebook messages with my student. Late Saturday night
mark the full moon effects. All the cats,
the tall experiment adds a nitrogen to fried to get a friend.
Apollo's lady pats the ground. Before she jumps

mark the full moon effects all the cats
of course. I kept her letters, and left them to the lion as marker in my will
tiger. Lily pads the ground, because she jumps
it's only a parsnip moon.

Hieratic VI

A chameleon
beached on a piece of paper
is bleached and dead trees

White chromatophores only background the foreground as we disguise poems in emails, a highly specialized clade of lizards. Let the coloring pattern continue to add meaning to nerve impulses and more. What is the golden ration of crickets and calcium powders? Let me be ultraviolet light, like epinephrine, not a parasite. White as platinum chameleon. Let the white travel from the nether layer to the melanophore layer to the chromatophore later to the epidermis. Treasure, like chameleon, comes from the word to lie to be situated to be in or at a place.

Idea with Her Spatula

bread and eggs and thread
and red eggs and glass red eggs

thread through the body
the beads and blood red orange

against the plastic
read for measure ring around

the volume something
for lifting and turning fish

golden and over
the wooden broad sword handle

and red cured and salt
cured idea and threaded

and turned the toast and
the roe spread read throughout bread

Transcript of the Hieratic

Oh my god in black ink, how did this pinecone get so big? The word elephant became equivalent to elegant in the head so mind the pinecone among the candles. In deed, the elegant sloth. Let me be an epiphyte, let us not repeat fine, if forest green is hunter green with blue here. Teeth are less interesting than language and trunks. The prehensile lips of horses can at least separate corn from sweet feed the picky eaters. The oldest cow is known as the matriarch of the group. Sit and whisper down the lane to sanity: one guinea pig, two guinea pigs, no more guinea pigs. Pinecones must be cooked to be fed to guinea pigs. Think from a modified leaf.

golden larch and fir
in Fibbonacci numbers
bract scales or seed scales

METABOLIC AND COMMUNITY SYNERGY OF ORAL BACTERIA IN COLORECTAL CANCER

Kaitlin J. Flynn, Nielson T. Baxter, and Patrick D. Schloss

Gut Things I

The oral, at the end of one symbiosis is periodontopathic, we think parasitic bacterium to the human we think (symbiosis does not mean only parasitism to the) Fusobacterium nucleatum who has been, (like soybeans to breast cancer repeatedly and broadly) associated with parasitism within colorectal tumors.

"The oral periodontopathic bacterium Fusobacterium nucleatum has been repeatedly associated with colorectal tumors."

Hieratic VII

Metaphor is the tree, the vehicle to the tiger orchid tenor. Air plants, orchids are a high erratic plant, an epiphyte. Epiphytes go in the cracks of their host trees, where the compost falls and collects. They grow out of organic debris: trace the minerals lost, leaves shaped like haiku, pull the moisture away. The compost pile is a blooming buzzing profusion. The roots of orchids are highly specialized. Their old and dead epidermis cells are called the velamen, in part spongy and fibrous bodies. So the silver, white, or brown roots take inside the humidity; beauty is an emergent property. Gods are in the eye of the beholder. Eye of the stem, node, undeveloped bud is the beginning of growth again. The tree is the god of the tiger orchid. The growth pattern of the tree is the same as the human nervous system. Life history: I flower you.

Gut Things II

I am molecular in response to the time frame the analysis has identified the directions do not fight the specific the virulence will fall to almonds, lemons, glass oh my; the Romulans will almost by themselves be the factors that promote this tumorigenesis because it has been waiting in the colon for millennia alone.

"Molecular analysis has identified specific virulence factors that promote tumorigenesis in the colon."

Gut Things III

Who however other than the Romulans? the oral at the end of community, for millennia alone members for millennia alone, such as members of the Porphyromonas spp., they are also equals if so found with F. nucleatum themselves on and on colonic tumors, and thus, narrow studies of the individual humanoid path of the next generation pathogens; they do not take community-wide and dire, die here virulence of the Romulan-Human conflict (properties into) account: Tam had told tin man the Romulans were dangerous.

"However, other oral community members, such as members of the Porphyromonas spp., are also found with F. nucleatum on colonic tumors, and thus, narrow studies of individual pathogens do not take community-wide virulence properties into account."

Gut Things IV

A broader view of boiled and peeled almond fangs, thinks of oral bacterial physiology and the things of the next generation pathogenesis, that identifies with two fingers two factors that could promote colonization (and not shun binding to teeth with) persistence, being bridges, they are those of drivers of oral bacterial communities who will bond do bond, did bond in the colon since its isolation was millennia alone.

"A broader view of oral bacterial physiology and pathogenesis identifies two factors that could promote colonization and persistence of oral bacterial communities in the colon."

Gut Things V

Tam calls for the polymicrobial nature of oral, for all to form biofilms, telepathic and not specific to the asaccharolytic (oh no picnic) metabolism of many Romulans, of these species, make them a consortium of one another, well suited to the wall in life, when in the microenvironment of the almond and the milk of the almond known as tin man, humankind, colonic lesions.

"The polymicrobial nature of oral biofilms and the asaccharolytic metabolism of many of these species make them well suited to life in the microenvironment of colonic lesions."

Hieratic VIII

as rabbits are pawns
not yet queens, not parasites,
impossibly white

Gut Things VI

Consideration of these orchid flowers two factors, his fingers sank into the walls offers a novel perspective on the role of the traveling bear, to be oral microbiota and Betazoid Humanoid in the initiation, tree in development, and tin man may commit suicide after Tam dies at the end of one symbiosis, millennia alone, treatment is instinct, the treatment of colorectal cancer is.

"Consideration of these two factors offers a novel perspective on the role of oral microbiota in the initiation, development, (tin man may commit suicide after Tam dies) and treatment of colorectal cancer."

Re: MISSION

Re: Permission, Mission Statements, and Through

dear: rabbit to do(e)
sure: as insurance for mortality, of course, and never loss
of use
if there is etiquette: there are twins
but:
you: the gold rabbit
you should: conditions all the rabbits between Alba and shadow
share: do the four toads
copies: coping with {with}
with those you knew who knew that: the point is white
fluorescent blue light
you knew that: you need that
person: one Flemish giant rabbit

{fight} what about the fourth horse? how did we forget
about the fourth horse? the hand me down horse means
theme means money.

I wish you all the warmth of a heavy weight horse
blanket.

ps. Olga and I want to know if you would do a headstand
if we collaborate again?

The Pawns are Drones, Simple Cylinders with Tiny Funereal Beaks and Dull Dud Dotted Eyes.[1]
written with Olga Kolesnikova

you had better not
steal touch from unseen fingers
your shame will last yet

The knight will rear yellow-white with age, my oldest-youngest friend spring into the game.
Beware of Quaker pedagogy. The board could be plotted in algebraic notation. Against the wazir means inverted rook where rabbits are horses with big ears and fragile leg bones. Carve the bones and cover with varnish. Queens are clever and slippery and the mothers of all rabbits. Once upon a time, the ocean was as full of whales as the field was of rabbits, remember the voyage home. Carve the bones, paint with ribbons of blood, and cover with varnish. I am trying to get it less wrong with experimental pieces: nightrider, knightmare, and unicorn mean inverted knight. One of my ambitions is to be king of the rabbit poems. In passing is the only time a piece is captured without its square being conquered by a pawn. Pawns are promoted for reaching their journey's end, and yet return again. Vague and fuzzy ideas multiply like rabbits. The valley of the rabbits echoes with what else could we do about our dead rabbits?

mean, soft Dutch bunny
bobo, you were almost mine.
blood on white snow, rats.

syllables castles
chess pieces carved from rabbit
read the ivory

---

[1] From SJ Fowler's "the Bocklin Garden: Part II" *Red Museum* (Newton-le-Willows: KFS, 2011)

Even in the summer the sun goes away. These lanes are treacherous so do consider your next move. In that pile of human waste we found children's toys and needles disguised as pens, but the infected needles are not the only carriers of disease. Go through the barbed wire arch and into the tetanus fields, where blind rabbits dance with the myxoma virus. It all feels a little funny in the early mornings, when the horses still sleep and teenagers exchange sexual favors in the shrubbery. The rabbit head without a body, the drowned rabbit with its feet tied up – we fished it out and laid it down to rest. The hunters will come out, the hunters will entice them, they will lay them down side by side and take school photos, it is like they have never been awake. Even at birth they were called litter.

wizard sent to men
and elves with rabbit drawn sleigh
Radagast will fight

Receiving Permission to Give Permission
BY SJ FOWLER

dear: black rabbit to red eyes
sure: as life insurance, of course, and never use of loss
if there was etiquette: there are twins, one is gone.
but:
you: the white rabbit
you should: conditions all the rabbits between borders
and shadows
share: do the four frogs
coping: copies with {without}
with those you know who know what: the point is black
opaque blue light
you know that: you don't need that
person: one welsh tiny rarebit

{recede} what about the fourth bear? how did we forget
about the fourth bear? the hand me down bear means
powder means house.

I wish you all the warmth of a heavy weight bear
blanket.

ps. Olga and yourself should collaborate. but i am unable
to headstand. if there's a chance to put you two on
together, i shall share it

May the Strawberries be with You All the Ways.

Dear oldest youngest friend, today is the day of the
strawberries and they will turn into pumpkins if not eaten
before midnight, you must understand having older
parents and no ponies.
The gray-green mold means older fruit here.
What happens to the champagne when garnished with a
green bear?
            What bonds can be preserved?
                        This is a glycosidic bond.
This a bond standing in the stead of dread and pear cider.
So the oxidizing agent plus fuel plus oxygen yields
carbon plus water plus carbon dioxide plus energy.
Beautiful means the purple flames coming from the once
gold, once green bear in the test tube in the fume hood in
the poem.

Receiving the Missing is Against the Everyday

dear: witch man
sure: as this was the summer of labradorite and sepsis and waiting
if there was etiquette: better dead than coed
but:
you: stayed until the dark blue lantern year
you should: buy more candles
share: four frogs equal two rabbits, pewter and palladium at meanwhile farm
coping: with giants and chinchillas
with those you know who know that: the point grows
you know: you need that grandmother
person: you are if you can eat cheddar and mustard on bread on Monday

I wish you all the warmth of a rabbit held in each of your
elbows.

{borders everyday} what is lost without the bear? did we forget or did
we forfeit the sour apple gummy bear without the powder? the bear
means the tree means Newtonian physics.

ps. if Olga and I translate the third line of chemotherapy
for a triple negative metastatic breast cancer patient, will
you give us to learn to headstand as a reward for our
poem? We have lambs and rabbits and rats so far.

Ant Bear could be an aardvark, could be a giant anteater known to defend its territory and when asleep it appears to be real.

Here lies the grandmother of the fur tea-cosy, better known as Myrmecophaga tridactyla; it is especially vulnerable to fires as it moves slowly and wears a flammable coat.

It rests in the forest, the body of the teapot lets itself cool down while resting and heat up for foraging ants like tea leaves, like black sapphires, like sand grains for tongue to make fluid for the anteater to drink.

Here comes the formic acid produced by the ants to aid in their own digestion; where there is tea, there is the bear who would hold, see the holding pattern, the giant honey colored rabbit.

Keynote

i will give you: paclitaxel known as taxol is always the answer
learn: that albumin bound paclitaxel comes
to headstand for: key and true the white rabbit says
this yes: you write like a chemist

if: insulted
a headstand can be: the third is not given to turn
a crab: into a bear
back: to the faith implicit in doubt
bridge: the body of the x marks witch

Hieratic IX

Duck rabbit,
dear first rabbit
residing in the vase of ambiguous figures.

Duck duck pair, whenever
two of us meet,
we must say something nice. About a third,
insert Quaker pedagogy here:
minding the light gives
teaching to learn/learning to teach.
Meditations on the classroom takes

duck duck frog, not at all.
You are nobodies frog; the third duck is not
given   what the duck?
          What the French/ toast, no waffle fries.
          What the fjord? horse the height of a pony and
not too drafty.

Duck duck duck duckling apples fall
it is their life goal. Life history:
we all desire oxygen oxygen carbon. We hate it.

Life goal: silence will fall.
This is not your mother's deacreation;
that oldest spelling mistake see here. Friend,
steal this classroom, dear quacker
run quicker around the circle.

Quicker, quack, quake (life goal) silence will fall
from duck, duck, duck, duck, duck, mallard and all.

HEARING KINGS
AND FROGS

Hope in Saltwater

there is no god of
the day today, walk the dog
whelks, you are welcome

To the mid tidal zone, to the middle shore come those gray foraging gods, see the great orange-brown of bromine, see those gastropods your rock snail family. Make a bowl of bread for yourself, and I will let the dog winkle be well fed. If you take the predator for a Chinese frying pan, the dog whelk can break the soft body down and so often turns the mussel into a tissue soup.

You are well to come.

Take the dog winkle for a walk in the margins, these mussels do not play, they prey with thread on the predator that walks through their beds. These byssal threads are a measure of defense against the dog whelks. Attack is heard as attach here. The threads come to hold the snail animal immobile, this holding pattern leads to death. Mussels pray for humans to make more red, purple, and violet dyes because they are heard under water to mean read purple violent deaths for the whelks.

Hope in Freshwater

me glochidium
you are what you eat minnow
and trout and salmon

You are what you steal into the freshwater from the forest of host fish rushing through the forest of trees. The larva are the little butterfly clips of these parasite bodies of almost mussels released from the gills of the female mussel into the river into the gills of the host fish. The host is the fish who will grow a blanket of cells over the larvae, inside this cyst they will stay for a month or so. So much time depends upon the river water temperature. Mussel larvae are not quite epiphytes and not quite parasites, and yet, please let me be a epiphyte not a parasite.

Hieratic Respiration

fish the habitat
be a traveling larva
be a parasite

The larva will fall to the bottom of the body of water, clean means sediment without silt or pity. On a scale from one to ten, how bad is the pain? I will give one-third of myself to the freshwater to the pursuit of oxygen. You are what you steal here is a salmon colored stethoscope from the big hill hospital; do not ask me about hope. There is no god of the day today, the goal is singular, where my guardian angel means my gift from the science gods. Here is high erratic resolution; you are welcome too.

High Erratic Inspiration

pleural effusions
excess fluid exudate
needle take its fill

For chest see the chicken breast bedside the ultrasound machine. Slide the head of the transducer against the gel against the skin as it sends out ultrasound waves in the body travel fastest through through bone. The speed of sound returning is translated into different organs on the screen. The fluid surrounding the lungs is what we are listening for the blackness surrounding the days. Let me be an epiphyte, let us not repeat fine if forest green is hunter green with blue here, the blue protocol does not obtain. Beside: one bronchus leads to smaller bronchi leads to smaller bronchioles leads to smaller alveoli leads to smaller slices of the peach. Let the vehicle be the needle through the grey-pink tissue because the new Tappan Zee Bridge is beautiful.

Animalia, Chordata, Vertebrata
After Wilfred Franklin

Being unpacked from the box, handed from him to her, and held. She names me neither Lithoabtes catesbeianus nor Rana pipiens, but Fred. Free will is almost reduced to tears. She touches her lips to my slippery back and hands me into the cleanest pond I will ever know. The waterfall, the ripples, free will calls her a pacifist sociopath. She hands William into my pool. Another true frog, flattened pyriform body of the problem, amphibia, anura, ranidae. The professor will pour alcohol into me until I am time-traveling.

Free will is dissected instead. No introductory biology student will slice into my abdomen with a half rusted scalpel. I dream of old frogs growing into rich food for orchids. I dream of trees with ponds of dirty water.

High Fantasy

Enough is enough fentanyl to sleep to death, does the patient concur? Does the daughter concur? Asks the voice of the creator's wife. The voice of the computer who fell in love with the shapeshifter. I am Commander Riker. I am playing the part of the second in command. Summer solstice is when I will have grown a beard. The big green is when I will marry the Betazoid who taught me to speak my mind.

Shape These Things
After Annabel Banks

One and a half pounds of squid were cleaned, their skin was removed, and their bodies cut into one quarter inch rings. The tentacles were reserved for another purpose. The Roma tomatoes had been diced and were slippery. The garlic cloves had been smashed by her, she remembers gloves and punching bags in miniature.

The olive oil, garlic, and crushed red pepper flakes had been added to a large sauté pan. The heat was turned to medium high. As the garlic had become fragrant, the tomatoes, oregano, and salt were added and the contents of the pan were stirred. The mixture was cooked until the tomatoes released their tears. The white wine was added to deglaze the pan. When the wine had begun to be reduced, the squid was added to the pan. It was cooked until it had become opaque.

Meanwhile, a large pot of salted water was brought to a boil. The squid ink linguine was added and cooked for two to three minutes. Afterwards, starch and salt and water were pulled through the colander. The black linguine and two tablespoons of pasta tears were added to the sauté pan. Then parmesan, grated not shaved, and more olive oil were added and gently tossed about. The magic would come in the form of fresh oregano.

When plated, the linguine had absorbed less sauce liquid than tagliatelle would, because it had less surface area. Steep was the hill of pasta, tomato, squid, oregano, and parmesan had dusted the peak. It had filled the plate. The fork was turned against the soup spoon, the black cables were being turned by it until it screamed.

There has Always Been a Pew at Cape Wrath
Jeanette Winterson

A phorophyte holds its orchids in the light. There, minding the light, lived the blind lighthouse keeper. My storyteller lived at the most north-westerly point in mainland Scotland, the old Norse turning point. In the time of Robert Stevenson the light was a paraffin lamp with red and white reflectors. The first light was replaced by a mercury vapor lamp, replaced by a temporary electrical power beam, replaced by a gear-less pedestal and lamp array system. A pew will hold its humans in the light; the wood still cares for me though the tree is dead. Cape Wrath was converted to automatic status on March 31 1998; and is now remotely monitored from the Northern Lighthouse Board's offices in Edinburgh.

the sky turns silver
dear ghost of the present tense
with the morning rain

LET THERE BE A BEAR
AND A LISTENER

Let There Be a Tree Plus a Plant.

in front of upon
prior to on, indicate
position over

To place us inside this discussion, ecology, and hierarchy, some pre-positioning is necessary as well as many prepositions. Epiphytes are plants that grow on, grow out of other plants in a mutual or commensal relationship; epiphytes are not parasites. The etymology of the two terms is illustrative, epiphyte: in addition, plant and phorophyte: to bear along plant. Let us begin with the biological concept of mutualism as a metaphor for collaboration, where our two poets are plants. Mutualism is a type of symbiotic relationship between individuals of two different species that is beneficial for both. It can be contrasted with parasitism, a symbiotic relationship between two individuals of different species where one individual benefits and the other is harmed. Mutualistic relationships between different species of plants can be characterized in further detail. Such relationships occur in both marine and terrestrial environments. Epiphytes are plants that grow upon other plants; they receive physical support, improved access to sunlight. The hosts of epiphytes are phorophytes and they receive shade and moisture from their plants. By means of this bi-directional exchange, the participants in a mutualistic relationship both receive the ingredients they need to live. When one poet is the phorophyte and the other poet is the epiphyte, they both receive the ingredients they need to write a poem.

When one doctor is the phorophyte and the other patient is the epiphyte, they both receive the ingredients they need to write a poem. If by poem, we mean lines of writing, then lines of chemotherapeutic agents given to the patient by the doctor, lines mutually agreed upon become the transcripts of their bi-directional exchange. 'This view of medical discourse as a dialectic between the voice of the lifeworld and the voice of medicine is thus linked by Mishler to a more general societal conflict of representation: 'the technocratic expressed through a language of purposive-rational action, and the symbolic expressed through ordinary language'. This dialectic can be further refined by employing the characterizations of figurative language from literary theory. The doctor is reading the patient both the part of the patient that is presenting the symptoms and the whole person; practicing medicine in this way is parsing synecdoche. Synecdoche is only one example of metonymy. 'From the perspective of synecdoche, the actions of metaphor and metonymy are not opposed to one another, but rather work together to pull parts out of, and put them back into, wholes. They invite us to attend to them, to dwell in them, to make them live. As forms of language that call attention to themselves, metaphors, metonyms and synecdoche estrange us from what we think we know.' Metonymies are high erratic thoughts not hierarchies at all. They are constantly reframing the boundaries of what we know we know and what we know we do not know. Metaphors are hierarchical only in the sense that they reframe our knowledge of ourselves; the vehicle carries what the reader knows over to what is not known to the reader. Like the hair of a shedding bear, like the leaves falling from a tree, let us move between metaphor and metonymy.

We will proceed through a series of metaphors, where each new metaphor changes one character or one relationship; the metaphors will cascade. Metaphors are a type of figurative language that transfer the concrete experience of the vehicle into the abstract and previously unknown tenor. As the tenor of the first metaphor is made familiar to the reader, it will become the vehicle of the next metaphor. We will present and participate in a journey, not only linearly through the essay and poetry and performance, but through a self-referential series of metaphors derived from the performance and my interpretation of the performance. My interpretation will be interdisciplinary, beware. 'Interdisciplinary conversations are exercises in explaining to one another the multiple ways in which we are 'metaphorizing' our individual metonymic landscapes, seeking and articulating the shape of the paths we take through them and the habits we have formed to traverse them. Even more profoundly, we are learning not only how to illuminate different items in these landscapes, and how to take different routes among them, but-to extend the metaphor we use so frequently here-to consider how we might actually rearrange the territory, to use one another's metaphors to alter our own metonymic landscapes.'

We begin located within the metonymic landscape of a forest with epiphytes and phorophytes. Our landscape is grounded in mutualism in pair relationships. 'Grappling with the metaphors of another challenges and changes our own metonymic landscapes, which in turn alters our own metaphors, which may in turn alter others'. The resulting path of exploration may indeed be more of a meta-path than a clear path as it privileges the breadth of the distance traveled over the depth of discussion. This discussion may be an essay-poem hybrid, essay is taken to mean that which elucidates and poem is taken to mean that which edifies. As elucidation and edification are both aims of interpretation, there is some necessary overlap between the two, that this piece is purposefully exploring. Therefore, this discussion will attempt to incorporate creative and critical elements at the level of form as well as content.

As a poetic form that traditionally takes travel as its subject and a combination of haiku and prose as its form, the haibun is ideally suited to this project. The haibun form can be interpreted as the meaning of metaphor translated into poetic form. We will explore a specific formulation of the cancer is a journey metaphor; cancer is a journey through the forest. As metaphors consist of two elements in conversation, so do haibun; they consist of any number of haiku and prose poems. The haiku's spare appeal to the senses aligns with the vehicle of the metaphor. The prose's complication of the haiku aligns with tenor of the metaphor. Haibun are comparable to metaphors at the formal level, where the haiku carries over its concrete appeal to the senses onto the more abstract prose, generally. The relationship between epiphytes and phorophytes is metaphorical; the trees hold the plants up to the light; the plants are raised over the forest floor by the trees. However, the content of the haibun may interact in more complex patterns because the poems are not limited to a single haiku and prose pairing.

In our exploration, we will deploy a domino effect of metaphors, falling one after another into place and landscape in the form of haibun. Haibun vary in length: the shortest being a haiku and a single sentence, the longest being as long as the longest work of literature. It is in this repetition of the elements of metaphor within the context of a coherent piece that the haibun becomes a series of metaphors in the same way that our exploration does. Our exploration will rely on concrete imagery at the beginning of every section; it is, a double a hybrid, a critical haibun. Let us discover what is lost without a bidirectional exchange between medicine and poetry? Collaboration is important to the practice of both poetry and medicine, and therefore, it is worth exploring how it is deployed in these two disparate fields as forests of knowledge.

poems multiply
centimeters of roots grow
tall experiments

Let us begin in fungi, as fungi we are interconnected, we find ourselves on the floor of a forest, we communicate silently as a polite audience of poets does. Our freckles, are they just dirt that has dropped from a hiker's boot or an air plant's root? What is similar across bears and orchids? Need. The need for others and to need is to speak to others and speech can by overheard. We watch the bear approach his needs. The bear is lumbering down the path between the trees; the bear and the mushrooms are still silent. Wedding march slowly, we are reminded that a bear cannot marry a tree. We become impatient with this waiting room. The tree, because there is only one tree now who is not waiting but reordering its leaves in anticipation of the interview. This tree is a mess, littered with leaves all over itself. Impossibly, many palms to read in order to predict the future here. These leaves should not be shuffled so often, the cards are already random, the tree is the dealer. He needs, the bear needs to know his cards now and the bear feels the delay is intolerable. The bear gives the forest the finger. Turning his back on the tree and the fungi, the bear looks to the sun and interprets the spots before his eyes as windows. What he sees could be his future, could be cardiology test results, could be music recording software. The bear stares down the diagnosis, itself part of the diagnostic encounter.

Let There Be a Poet Under a Tree.

in the direction
of down too, in advance of
two in order to

Roots present the bear with a chair and the bear seats himself. What are eyes but blemishes in the skin? Blue him wishes into the holes in the tree trunk, they are eye to eye. The branches of the tree grow in the direction of the bear as the bear leans into the trunk of the tree. They come eye to eye again as if they could listen to their blemished wishes, as if symmetry is enough to make things come true. The bear stares, the tree stares back though they differ as doctors from patients do. There is a symmetry in action here.

Time is a microphone for what trees would say if mammals would listen. Just over there, see time holding up the voice of the tree for the whole forest to hear. Time finds the underside of chin. Time knows the anatomy of trees better than the bear, but time knows the chest of the bear and settles there. Authority is a kind of time. Who has the higher author, the tree or the archeologist? The tree may tower over the archeologist when it is young and the archeologist may look down to read the dead tree. The science of reading information about a forest from its tree trunks is known as dendrochronology and is a valuable methodology for archeologists. The tree would be the record. Look at the words heart wood and listen to the body of the tree undulating. Ring around the years. The dendrochronologist's pockets are empty of leaves, empty of flowers, empty of seeds. What burned to ashes is what burned down. What is left? Let the tree be happy with the poetry.

comes from tupelo
family camptotheca
acuminata

The parent camptothecin comes from the bark. Topotecan has greater solubility in water due to the basic side chain at carbon nine. (Like dissolves like deoxyribonucleic acid.) It's nitrogen is a Lewis base. The rest of this pentacyclic lactone is fused flat system of rings extensively conjugated. Planes are essential to intercalating agents (the poet is an intercalating agent). These pi bonds help Topotecan slip in between the DNA bases.

It's action is synthesis phase see DNA replication specific.

The bulky substituents on the benzene ring do not hinder binding (his tongue intercalates itself between the pages despite the bulky substituent that is his head). Topoisomerase I binds to DNA, DNA binds to Topotecan, Topotecan binds to Topoisomerase I. The formation of this ternary complex interferes with the movement of the replication fork and induces replication arrest. It causes a double stranded DNA break. Then apoptosis happens. The breaking project again learning from extinctions and life.

Happily comes apoptosis.
Happily comes cell death.

Let There Be a Bear Before a Tree.

mass of the body
meet the flora and fauna
teeth experiment tall

Bears utilize trees for communicating with other bears; they bite and claw the trees to leave visible marks as well as rubbing against the trees to deposit scent and hair to show their presence to other bears in the area. This written on the tree presence, helps bears maintain their territorial claims and find potential mates. Bears will also use utility poles for the same purpose.

suborder of dog-
like creatures, they look un-bear-
like long tails long teeth

Let us define collaboration as nothing more than a bidirectional exchange between the two collaborators. If there is not symmetry to the exchange, there must at least be reciprocity; an active form of listening that consists of hearing and voicing a response that either reflects or refracts what the speaker has communicated. The bear is orbiting the tree. Communication between the two contains elements of symmetry and complementarity. The tree directs the path of the bear.

Let There Be a Poet After a Bear.

teeth against tree lost
bark writing bear lost black hair
fades to blond bird's nest

Bear is Chrissy Williams first full length collection published by Bloodaxe 2017. The image of bears recurs throughout the poems, functioning as both image and theme. The bear appears as the vehicle in multiple metaphors where the tenor varies. For example: the bear is the heart, the bear is the poet, the bear is the wild, the bear is love, and much more. In order to more fully explore the role of the bear as the poet in this collection let us focus ourselves on two poems: 'Bear of the Artist' and 'The Lost.'

'Bear of the Artist'

I asked the artist to draw me a heart and instead he drew me a bear.
I asked him, 'What kind of heart is this?' and he said, 'It's not a heart at all.'
I asked him, 'What kind of bear is this?' and he said, 'It's not a bear either.'
I asked him, 'What kind of artist are you anyway?' and he said,
'I am the one who exists to put bears in your head, who exists
to put ideas in your head in place of bears, who mistrusts anyone
who tells you they know what kind of place the heart is, the head,
how it should look, what size, what stopping distances, etc.
and as long as you keep me existing to put bears in your head,
I will, because nights are getting darker, and we're all tired,
we're all so tired, and everyone could use a bear sometimes,
everyone could use a wild bear, though they can be dangerous
and there's nothing worse than a bear in the face, when it breaks –
always remember how your bear breaks down
against the shore, the shore, the shore.'

As the first poem in the collection, let us take this poem to be defining the role for both the poet and the bear throughout the rest of the poems in the book. Although this poem suggests that the poet is not themselves the bear, but the creator of the bears, let us believe that the poet does become the bear when performing the bear poems. This self-referential work creates a complex a series of frames within frames for the interpreter of Williams' collection. With this idea of the poet performing the bear performing the poem, the discussion will turn towards 'The Lost'. This poem does not directly mention any bears, and presents a collage of Italian to English translations of the first three lines of Dante's *Inferno*. The original three lines are the epigraph to the poem followed by three stanzas, each devoted to rearrangements of those same three lines. The effect of this almost repetition is two-fold first to invoke a sense of disorientation; the reader is literally going in circles, seeing the same signs and signifiers of meaning again and again without progressing. Second comes a sense of anticipation, something is about to come, meaning is about to return to the poem. At the end of "The Lost" the reader is eagerly anticipating the return of direction of new ideas of guidance. For those familiar with Dante's text, their thoughts will turn to Virgil the poet who guides the narrator through the circles of hell. For those familiar with only William's text, their thoughts will turn back to the first poem, "Bear of the Artist," which also characterizes the poet. Combining these two interpretations, leads the reader to see Dante as the artist who drew the bear and Virgil as the bear. While this statement may sound absurd, it is important bear in mind the meaning is not absolute, but it determined by context. 'Meaning is not a thing; it involves what is meaningful to us. Nothing is meaningful in itself. Meaningfulness derives from experience of functioning as a being of a certain sort in an environment of a certain sort.' Williams has made new meaning in a canonical text, by placing it in a novel environment, a forest; she has translated it into a conversation on ecology. This is an example of a translation as an interpretation of the text, without changing the language in which the text is written. Williams is a translator as interpreter of text and creator of a new text in response to the original is a poet.

until in spite of
close to continuously
before the coming

Susan Sontag makes the image of the poet as a bear literal in a photograph taken by Annie Leibovitz. Sontag appears dressed in a teddy bear suit, complete with gloves and hat, sitting at her desk with a laptop open. In the black and white photograph she appears poised to type on the laptop, her fingers left unencumbered by the costume. This image can be interpreted as the picture equivalent to one thousand of the words she has written about photography. Sontag writes that 'surrealist manipulation or theatricalization of the real is unnecessary, if not actually redundant. Surrealism lies at the heart of the photographic enterprise: in the very creation of a duplicate world, of a reality in the second degree, narrower but more dramatic than the one perceived by natural vision... Surrealism has always courted accidents, welcomed the uninvited, flattered disorderly presences.' The presence of a bear at a laptop recalls accounts of bears wandering into campsites and cabins on the one hand; and writers disguise themselves in their works. The writer as the bear is wandering into stranger spaces and making themselves at home. The bear and the human camper at the edge of the forest are meeting in a liminal place; the boundary between wild and civilization; they are both in the feral place. The expression on Sontag's face is sad and weary; it is an image of the state that the narrator of the *Inferno* uses to describe himself. Sontag has two entangled identities in this image; 'essentially the camera makes everyone a tourist in other people's reality, and eventually in one's own.' Annie Leibovitz is the creator of the reality of this photograph as Dante is the author of the *Inferno*.

notwithstanding on
the road to pointing to through
position en route

Let There Be a Veterinarian Near a Bear.

headed for here
the heart is a noisy bear
nose the hibiscus

Let us listen to the heart first of a human as a bear then of a bear as a human. In order to listen to the mammalian heart, not as a poet, but as a practitioner of medicine, a stethoscope is required. A binaural stethoscope consists of a bell, a diaphragm, and tubing. The bell is a hollow cup that transmits low frequency sounds to the listener's ears; while the diaphragm is a plastic disc that transmits high frequency sounds. The tubing carries the acoustic vibrations of body sounds to the ears of the listener. Stethoscopes may be used to listen to the heart, the lungs, and the gastrointestinal tract of large and small animals. The stethoscope is no more than a refined microphone and earphone combination. Kiwan Sung utilizes a combination of earphones and microphone placed over Fowler's heart in order to amplify, listen to and record his heartbeat. He is performing the role of a veterinarian as Fowler performs the part of the bear. The veterinarian is caring for the bear; the bear is under the care of the veterinarian. The two creatures are positioned with respect to another. The stethoscope is itself a metaphor because it bridges the distance, allowing the veterinarian to listen to the bear's heartbeat as though his head were pressed to the bear's chest. The length of the stethoscope tubing is determined by the desired distance from the patient; the larger and more dangerous the patient, the longer the tubing. For example, infants and lizards would take the shortest length of tubing. Bears and other large animals would take the longest length of tubing to give as much space as possible between animal and human. This human desire for distance, this medical desire for distance is in fact what inspired the invention of the stethoscopes by the nineteenth century French doctor Laënnec.

via with a view
to facing with respect up
to each approaching

'Laënnec was reluctant to start immediate auscultation (placing the doctor's ear on the patient's chest) because of the age, sex and plumpness of the patient. In this moment of embarrassment, Laënnec recalled his observation of the children's wood borne signaling. It was this observation that inspired Laënnec's invention of the stethoscope.' His account of his motivation for inventing the stethoscope is at once brilliant and problematic. The stethoscope provides physicians with a superior access to the sounds of the patient's heart, and therefore, facilitates diagnosis. The stethoscope may be characterized as bridging the distance between the doctor's ear and the patient's heart. Oh the other hand, the stethoscope introduces a physical distance between the doctor's ear and the patient's heart; it acts as an intermediary between the two humans in much the same way as a telephone does. Without the stethoscope, percussion and auscultation were used to listen to fluids in the patient's heart and lungs. Both of these methods required the doctor to place their hands or head directly upon the patient. The stethoscope is positioned between the hand and head of the doctor and the chest of the patient.

In Laënnec's account, he is specifically resistant to listening the chest sounds of a female patient, and justifies the use of stethoscope as a tool to preserve female modesty. However, I would argue that this need to protect female modesty is simultaneously sexualizing the female body, implying that a woman's body can never be anything but a sexual object. This phenomenon is seen today in the language and prohibitions surrounding public breast feeding and the censoring of female, but not male nipples in images on the internet. The sexualization of the female body makes it as threatening to male professional as the body of the bear, because both are other. The male professional does not want to know the other, especially to have to come into physical contact with the other's body. The problem here is ironic: the person assigned and trained to respond to bodily problems is uncomfortable with the body of the patient and therefore turns the patient, whether man or woman or animal, into a bear.

Let us turn from the historical to present fantastic novel, *Memoirs of a Polar Bear*, which portrays a counter example to the bear as other to humans. The human character Mattias is charged with caring for baby polar bear, who was rejected by his mother. The baby polar bear, Knut, requires from his human zookeeper two kinds of nursing. Mattias is responsible for preparing Knut to see the veterinarian and assisting in the exam and treatment. Specifically, he must prepare the food and convince the polar bear to eat the food the veterinarian thinks best. This first type of nursing is determined by the desires and needs of the human veterinarian; the second type is determined by the desires and needs of the animal, Knut. 'How animals categorize depends on their sensing apparatus and their ability to move themselves and to manipulate objects.' The two characters have a doubly transgressive relationship that emerges from Mattias successfully performing the two kinds of nursing. The intimacy of the nurse patient relationship is shown in sharp contrast here to the doctor patient or veterinarian patient relationship.

bear is woman in
autumn man in spring heartbeat
found through fur and skin

Mattias is responsible for feeding, cleaning, and entertaining the baby polar bear everyday; he performs the role of mother bear. Knut describes Mattias as 'a true mammal, far more so than many of his sort, because he gave suck: he fed me not only milk but part of his own life. He was the pride of all mammals.' In this quotation we see, evidence an adoptive relationship that bridges the human-bear and male-female categories. We might call this relationship species-queer as well as gender-queer, where the notions of what defines an ideal bear or mother are carried over to Mattias. He embodies Knut's ideals.

As much as Mattias transforms into Knut's mother bear, Knut transforms into Mattias' human son; he becomes the protagonist of this section of the narrative. Knut becomes intelligible to the human reader, more and more human as the narrative progresses and the reader becomes invested in his life. 'In fact, the main character is never an animal. During the process by which an animal is transformed into a non-animal or a human into a non-human, memory gets lost, and it's this loss that is the main character.' It is ultimately Knut's loss of both his biological mother and his adopted mother that defines the narrative arch of his section of the text. The experience of loss is one that is as common to human as to bears; it carries over the definition of species.

Loss has the effect of locating one in relation to what it is that they have lost; it places them in a specific mental state: grief. 'Why is the measure of love loss?' asks the narrator of Jeanette Winterson's novel *Written on the Body*. This question is repeated, acting as a refrain in the prose creating a pattern, return to the mental state of grief. The grief is kept alive as the ghost of the loved one. Here is the grief of Paul Grobstein written as he explores his grief and we explore our grief through the frame of his grief; here is the half-life of Paul Grobstein.

> Every death is a break, a disruption in the established pattern of things for the survivors – whether they be species or languages or cultures or individual human beings or bacterial cells themselves. Evolution is when the plan no longer unfolds as it did. And is there something we could learn from the non-human world? We had some toads. Have we the naturalist fallacy that might be relevant to our reactions to sudden changes in the established patterns of things, that might ease our distress at them? Every retirement is a break, a disruption in the pattern of thinking and things.

the ghosts are roosting
let us learn from extinctions
and lifetimes and fights

If a feeling of loss is one (at least) of the important elements in our discomfort at breaking, maybe we need to examine that a little more closely. About 65 million years ago, the earth was struck by a large comet or meteor. In the ensuing cataclysm, something in the vicinity of 80% of existing species were lost. Extinction is when the pattern no longer exists.

Loss, in the sense of disappearance and disruption, lost was lost only in the narrowest sense. And maybe we could come to see disappearance not as loss but rather as a retirement, as a transformation, as a present ghost, perhaps acknowledge that what has lived beside us now lives inside us as the white rabbit. The professorial ghost resides in the back my head beyond tired things.

why is the measure
of love the loss of a bear
polar bear ghost bear

Enough is when the pattern can no longer hold us. Perhaps it is not actually having feelings, or even the feeling of being disturbed that causes us distress but the feeling of loss that does so? What is lost when words are wasted? Why are we so afraid of feeling tired? of letting athletes retire? leaving the boxing ring? the riding ring? Maybe it's not distress at loss and associated disruption that is the problem but rather a feeling of disruption that in turn produces a sense of loss?

Among those that survived were some small, furry animals that had changed little over the preceding million or so years. Following the cataclysm they began to more rapidly evolve and diversify, yielding today's boars and wolves and rabbits and whales. Ourselves watching the half-lives fall away as radioactive decay in the time of the white rabbit.

Enough is when the plan no longer holds our bodies. Enough to recognize that we are watching the half-lives fall away as rose petals in the time of the positron emission tomography scan. As we have always been, a part with other forms of life of a larger and ongoing experiment in trying out new ways of living.

to retire is just
to be tired it is time, it
rhymes, rose welcome home

Let There Be a Poet in Contemplation of an Oncologist.

in order to get
under the authority of
headed to through

There is a hierarchy in medicine that must be attended to, to ignore the hierarchy would result in high anarchy of treatment. To be a good doctor is to fit into the ecosystem, to function within the complexity. The medical director is higher than the head of department is higher than the attending physician is higher than the fellow is higher than the chief resident is higher than the senior resident is higher than the junior resident is higher than the intern is higher than the medical student. There is a parallel line for nursing staff. The chief nursing officer is higher than the director of nursing is higher than the nurse supervisor is higher than the clinical nurse specialist is higher than the charge nurse is higher than the registered nurse is higher than the licensed vocational nurse is higher than the unlicensed assistive personnel. Where each kind of medical practitioner is a kind of fauna or flora, the land of ill is a forest.

on the road to pro
for the sake of before just
before prior to

This metaphor gives a precise explanation for why doctors are the worst patients; they upset the hierarchy and are themselves upended in the grossest sense. It is less that any individual doctor could behave badly as a patient, it is that a doctor simultaneously occupying two positions in the hierarchy creates a paradox. At best, the doctor who is a patient redraws the linear hierarchy into a circular one (we may imagine that doctors imagine a circle of hell for themselves where doctors are treated as patients). To rephrase Sontag's description of the relationship between being ill and well yields, 'Illness is the night side of life, a more onerous citizenship. Every [doctor] who is born holds dual citizenship, in the kingdom of the well and in the kingdom of the sick. Although we all prefer to use the good passport, sooner or later each [doctor] is obliged, at least for a spell, to identify ... as citizens of that other place.'

so that one may as
far as in contemplation
in the direction of

The origin of the cancer is a journey metaphor; the patient must travel through the forest, perhaps circling, perhaps spiraling downwards, but always looking back towards the oncologist. See the specialists, the interventional radiologists, the surgeons for they are shrubs that the bear must forage every so often for nutrition and information. Circumnavigating the medical landscape, here is a portrait of a bear.

'Simple Gifts'

'Tis the gift to be simple, 'tis the gift to be free
'Tis the gift to come down where we ought to be,
'And when we find ourselves in the place just 'right,
'Twill be in the valley of love and delight.
'When true simplicity is gained,
'To bow and to bend we shan't be ashamed,
'To turn, turn will be our delight,
'Till by turning, turning we come 'round right.'

Here is a portrait of a tree. The tree is rightly patient, lying in vertical wait for the bear to return. The bear is the cancer patient. The bear dances with the tree taking up the entire stage. We are focused on the pair at the front of the stage, they are the foregrounded in any photograph of this environment. We the mushrooms must watch, we are bottom and background. This is the high erratic ecology of the ghost. The ghost is

in the irony
when a developmental
biologist dies

of ovarian cancer. The word written on the sticker on the bag of saline besides her name was topotecan. The passion of a toucan's feathers came from the decadron she took with it; her steroid induced ranting turning into lecture. I turned into her student. I studied how losing the pattern through tumorigenesis does recapitulate embryogenesis. Cancer is a result of development and evolution of life, of increasing complexity of body plans, of beauty (I write the most complex poems I can). Ovarian cancer is particularly aggressive because during development the cells to become germ cells must migrate a great distance, the cells remember, they are well traveled. What is the opposite of a ghost? (A poem or parsing cancer metaphors?) The descendants of these cells remember.

Let There Be a Poet Collaborating with Another Poet.

against through against
for against fronting against
facing off against

Let the poets doctor each other's work. Let them begin by listening to what is before them, to who is before them, let them begin in silence, and begin to fill in the silence of the other. The sounds begin to form a landscape. This soundscape will consist of SJ Fowler sounding out the constants of the English language with Kiwan Sung sounding out the vowels over and around the recording of both of their heart beats. The audience is located inside the brains and bodies of these two poets as they communicate. Human ears and brain usually background the sound of the movement of blood through its body, unless the sound is magnified with a tool such as a stethoscope. Fowler makes a circuit around the audience with the camera, note that most of the audience remains faced front observing Sung and the screen. He returns to sit down beside Sung again and continue their conversation; the difference in the sounds they make symbolize their individual differences as well as hint at their linguistic differences. Let us learn from listening to this performance.

with indicating
with results back for cancer
becoming ending

In our reading of this performance as an allegory of a collaboration between a doctor and a patient, the different sounds each poet vocalizes would symbolize medical discourse and colloquial speech respectively. The decision to divide the sounds in language between vowels and constants makes the complimentary nature of the sounds explicit. The voices of doctor and patient must come together to make sense; to make complex words and sentences and to deliver the entire narrative. Let us be clear, the narrative emerges from the conversation between the doctor and the patient; bidirectional exchanges can yield emergent results. To bring into the light the unforeseen occurrence, neither Fowler nor Sung intended their collaboration to speak to the doctor-patient relationship, and yet, as we have seen, they have created a powerful allegory for such a relationship through their collaboration. Let this performance be rewritten in the future.

with indicating
with results back for cancer
ending becoming

Reappearing

Let there be a plant listening to a tree.
Let there be a tree listening to a poet.

Let there be a tree listening to a bear.
Let there be a bear listening to a poet.

Let there be a bear listening to a veterinarian.
Let there be an oncologist listening to a poet.
Let there be a poet listening to a poet.

Notes:

http://www.americanmusicpreservation.com/SimpleGiftsmultimedia.htm

Gwyn, Richard, *Communicating Health and Illness* (London: Sage Publications, 2002) p. 71

Lakoff, George, *Women, Fire, and Dangerous Things: What Categories Reveal about the Mind* (Chicago: University of Chicago Press, 1990) p. 292

Lakoff, George and Johnson, Mark, *Philosophy in the Flesh* (New York: Basic Books, 1999) p.17

https://londonkoreanlinks.net/2017/05/18/event-news-beyond-words-south-korean-british-poets-in-collaboration/

https://www.ncbi.nlm.nih.gov/pmc/articles/PMC1570491/

https://www.ncbi.nlm.nih.gov/pmc/articles/PMC1570491/

https://www.nytimes.com/2005/12/04/magazine/illness-as-more-than-metaphor.html

https://www.ncbi.nlm.nih.gov/pubmed/11255861

https://www.theparisreview.org/blog/2012/05/15/susan-sontag-in-a-teddy-bear-suit/

https://serendipstudio.org/exchange/breaking/grobstein

https://serendipstudio.org/local/scisoc/DalkeGrobsteinMcCormack.html

http://www.stevenjfowler.com/blog/2017/5/12/a-note-on-south-korean-enemies-project-june-3rd-in-london

http://www.stevenjfowler.com/blog/2017/6/11/a-note-on-the-south-korean-enemies-project-was-very-cool

Sontag, Susan, *On Photography* (New York: Picador, 2001) pp. 52 and 57

Sontag, Susan, *Illness as Metaphor and AIDS and Its Metaphors* (New York: Picador 2001)

Tawada, Yoko, *Memoirs of a Polar Bear* (London: New Directions, 2016) pp.50 and 226

Williams, Chrissy, *Bear* (Hexham Northumberland: Bloodaxe Books Ltd, 2017)

Winterson, Jeanette, *Written on the Body* (New York: Vintage International, 1994)

https://www.youtube.com/watch?v=k0hWphtbd4Y